A Penitential Prayer

Poems on the Holocaust

Gerald George

Goose River Press
Waldoboro, Maine

Copyright © 2022 Gerald George

All rights reserved. No part of this book may be reproduced in any form without written permission from the publisher, except by a reviewer who may quote brief passages in a review to be printed in a newspaper or magazine.

Library of Congress Card Number: 2021953251

ISBN: 978-1-59713-241-1

First Printing, 2022

Cover photo by publicdomainpicture.net.

Published by
Goose River Press
3400 Friendship Road
Waldoboro ME 04572
email: gooseriverpress@gmail.com
www.gooseriverpress.com

Nazis declared that land within their control should be cleared of Jews and other "undesirables." Before they were stopped, six million people or more were separated from their families, their property, their livelihoods; subjected to humiliations, brutality, tortures, and killed with beatings, bullets, poison gas. *Six million.* This book is dedicated to them.

Acknowledgements

The following poems in this book were first published in *Goose River Anthologies 2019, 2020,* and *2021.* The author is grateful for permission to reprint them here: "Christmas!"; "Flowers Await"; "Love, Willie"; "O'er the Green Valley"; "Out of Order"; "So Many People"; "The Officer's Revolver"; "Was Something Wrong?".

Table of Contents

Your Dinner Awaits
Never Mind//1
Oh, Bosh!//2
Holiday//4
Perfection//6
Fired with Pride//8
Was Something Wrong?//9
Where?//10
In the Emptying Room//12
So Many People//13
Is He Dead?//14

Sleep, My Little Ones
Kiss Me Quick//19
A-Singing//21
The Truth//22
Freight Yard Telephone//23
Move!//24
Flowers Await//26

Table of Contents

A Matter at the Camp
The Officer's Revolver//29
Love, Willie//30
Out of Order//31
Peckity-Peck//32
Moment of Glory//33
Camp Cant//35
Shining Eyes//36
Purple and Gold//37
Christmas!//38

What's Left?
"I Join the Gulls"//43
Maximum Capacity//44
Dreams//46
"O'er the Green Valley"//48
Blood, Worms, Piss, Shit, Vomit//49
Revolt//51
Three Minutes//53
You Get Used to Anything//54
Black Smoke//56
In the Barracks//58

Table of Contents

A Penitential Prayer

Shivering in the Ditch//61
Then We'd Hear a Shot//62
Free?//63
Great Parade//65
Dung Buckets//66
Sewers//67
Why Ask Me?//68
Great Goethe//69
In Place of Explanation//70

Your Dinner Awaits

Never Mind

They all heard.
Coming from the woods
—the quiet, lovely forest—
dogs barking, screams, gunshots.

He couldn't stand not knowing.
He grabbed his shotgun, loaded it with shells.
"You'd better not go," his wife warned.
"Can we go too?" his children asked.

"Stay in the house," he ordered.
Then with a grim face
he took off walking rapidly
toward the forest.

After a while he reappeared,
weapon in hand, walking back.
The screams, the shots, continued.
"What is it? asked his wife.

"Never mind," he said.
"Just don't go near the forest ever again.
"You hear me?
"Never ever go."

Oh, Bosh!

Even after the family next door
had been forced to pack up,
deported to who knew where,
the neighbors noted a barberry bush
still grew in the back yard,

bright red.

The remaining neighbors often remarked
in casual chats with each other,
ordinary conversations when
no one unknown seemed likely to overhear,
Did you happen to notice . . . ?

brilliant red.

The red had started in pinkish orange,
seeming normal enough for the season,
but never before, according to Mrs. A,
talking with Mrs. B, who quickly agreed,
had the bush turned such an exceptionally

splendid red.

As Mrs. B said to Mrs. C, *You know,
it's, well, the color of blood, I mean,
not really, but, just a bit.*
Mrs. C mentioned this fact to Mrs. D,
I don't believe in such things, and yet . . .

exceptionally red.

Mrs. D told her husband, late in the day,
But of course we don't really think . . . .
He said, *Oh bosh!*, then called a friend,
an officer who sent soldiers over with spades
to dig the bush up and burn it down,

flaming red.

Holiday

A big door opened on a long parterre
offering a view of so many mountain peaks.
Officers strolled, chatted in small groups.
He lit a cigarette, contemplated.
Spectacularly beautiful, he mused to himself.
*This might have been the site where God
created the world . . . .*
He watched the sun make shadows
on the mountain sides, then heard the call
for the officers to return inside. He took
one last long look, then crushed his cigarette.

His mind kept lingering as the conference
resumed, the officer droning at the front,
statistics on the numbers who would need
to be dealt with. Could it be done?
Trains, stations, personnel required,
How many per day, potential bottlenecks,
How to keep the need for rations down?
Percentage who could work, how many hours?
They were getting down to answers now.
But along with all the doodles on his pad,
he had sketched a dozen mountain peaks.

In the train on the way home,
he studied the provisions for the prisoners
his unit would round up. Then mused awhile,
turning to a traveler's brochure.
He wondered if there might be a small, clean inn
out in the mountains where his family
could stay on holiday sometime.

But there would be so much to do before—
round up all the prisoners, pack them in
the railroad cars, and ship them off. Maybe
later there would be time for a holiday.

Perfection

Unrolling the scroll over the table,
the eager young architect explains his plan.
He has worked on it day and night
because they need it now.

Thousands will be housed
in three tiers of bunks
running up each side
of this interior space.
Long narrow barracks,
scores of them in rows.
Right down the middle
two sets of tracks.
Spaces on each side
for sorting into groups
– men, women, old, young,
feeble, and full-bodied.
Here's where their luggage goes.
Here for hair cutting.
Here for the shoes and boots.
Here's for all the clothing.
A big-enough space for every need.
Efficiency – maximum.

Men in suits who manage the plants
and uniformed troops who will run the camp
—he sees by the way they follow his words
that they are pleased with his work.
They will say yes to his plans.
He may even get an award!
Then one of them asks,
And the gas chambers?
He replies with a smile, *Right back here
with the crematoria.*

He will get his award.
He will build his camp and more.
He will get the thrill that comes
from perfect work.

Fired with Pride

O what a birthday! What a gift!
A uniform for a little lad
in brown and green with silver stars,
just like the one his father had.

How he strutted in his little boots,
swaggering as best he could
among the chairs of his parapet,
just the way his father would.

On his head a captain's cap
with a golden eagle at the fore,
to show he was an officer,
just like the badge his father wore.

O, how he longed to go to war,
armed with a rifle, fired with pride,
he looked so strong, so brave, so bold,
as did his father before he died.

Was Something Wrong?

She watched them drag her parents into the street,
made them take old toothbrushes to the grime
embedded in the stones by thousands of shoes,
then threw rocks through windows,
shattering the glass.
At first they didn't notice her standing there,
wondering what her family had done.

Was something wrong with how they'd baked the bread?
Had the fruit gone bad? Had some patron complained?
Had someone been short-changed?
If only the customer had told them what was wrong.
Why force her parents out?
What would warrant such mean treatment
as cleaning the old street?

Angry tears appeared upon her face.
This little place had been her only home,
full of comforting smells, where every day,
when school let out, she helped to keep the shop.
She ran outside, crying for her parents.
A uniformed guard quick-lifted his rifle-butt.
She never saw it coming.

Where?

He's reached the age of eighty-five.
He wishes to go nowhere.
His old bones can hardly bear
to get him in and out of bed.
What is this nonsense now about a train?

His son is urging him into his coat.
He daughter-in-law packs frantically.
The children look bewildered.
Two uniformed men await downstairs.
His son almost carries him step by step.

I'm not going!
The uniformed men hustle him out.
The family follows tight behind.
The cold wind chills his cheeks, his hands.
Where are we going? Where?

No response. He sees in the street
many of his neighbors with uniformed men
going somewhere. *Where? Where?*
He shakes with cold, confusion, pain.
He wants the warmth of his own bed.

The train station. All these people.
Cattle cars. *Where are we going?*
His son grabs his hand. It hurts.
Uniformed men push him up and in.
Jammed, crushed, he has to stand.

He cannot stand. All these people,
up against him, he can't breathe.
Hands around him hold him up.
He feels his urine starting to come.
Jammed tighter, great doors close.

Slowly close. The bolts slide shut.
After hundreds of miles, they'll open again
They'll find him, toss his body on a pile.
After a while, they'll burn it.
His last thought: the urine he couldn't control.

In the Emptying Room

I knew most of them—family, friends,
neighbors, people from the town—
all herded in the town hall, as if
we were there for a special holiday,
except the guards had guns.

They pulled out a few of us. The rest
they organized five abreast, sending them out,
down to the train station, so we were told.
I shivered a little, not knowing where they were going,
watching them all depart through the town hall door.

The thought came over me, standing in the emptying room,
that I might never see them again.
The guards took me—young and strong—out the back way
with the others they'd kept,
put us on a truck to the labor brigade.

Increasingly I felt empty, alone, afraid,
gripped with a sudden eruption of guilt.
Why didn't I break free, go to the others?
There were worse things than going down
in a barrage of bullets.

I would have a long time
to puzzle it out in the labor camp
while we slowly starved to death.

So Many People

... piled into the sorting camp from
different cities, waiting for the next
train out, days sometimes, trying
to make sense of it, the well-dressed
elderly woman who didn't want
to share her bunk with somebody from
a slum, or the beauty queen who set
up her compact mirror on a crate
to do her eyebrows before she had to go,
or the middle-aged man in tears,
sitting haphazardly in mud,
his wife and daughters already gone
while they held him for some kind of work,
or the old woman asking if she
could go home to fetch her medicine bottle,
could she go now? No? Oh—
and her new spectacles! Where
were they taking her? Why, why, why ... ?

Is He Dead?

I think he sneaked out of the ghetto. He
came to my house, he told me to come,
he wanted to show me, the ghetto, had
I seen it? Three fourths of the Jews had
already been taken away, but he wanted
me to see it. What could I do? He was so
insistent. He told me the ghetto wouldn't
be there much longer, that I must come
now, I had to see it for history's sake, I
had to see it to believe it. "Don't miss it,"
he said to me. "You can't let the ghetto go on
in your own time and not see it, not
know what it was like. Please, come on."

So I went, just for an hour. That's all I
promised, walked in, looked around.
He disappeared, then caught up with
me. Immediately I knew this was not my
world, not any world. Everybody left in
the ghetto, out on the street with an onion,
a cookie, a bit of clothing, whatever they
had, selling to each other, then begging when
they couldn't sell, women with babies to
feed, no breasts, just flat, babies crying,
babies with crazed eyes, children playing
with rags, throwing them at each other.
"Life goes on," he said with a smile. "No?"

"I want out," I begged. But he said, "Just
a bit more, look at this." a skeletal man
stood motionless next to a rickety tree,
didn't move. I asked, "Is he dead?" "Oh, no,"
he said. "But he's dying. Look at him, you
know him, you saw him—don't forget." We
moved on, saw more men, women." "What
are they doing here?" I asked. "Just dying,"
he said, "That's all, dying." "This is hell," I
said. "Oh, no," he replied. "Their agonies
will be over soon. They have death to look
forward to, sweet death. But now, I think
your dinner awaits. Please—just remember this."

Sleep My Little Ones

Kiss Me Quick

Just a few soldiers to force so many on the train.

The way she tosses her head when she's being saucy,
the giggle in her voice, the sexy smile,
the laughter in her look,
the curve of her lithe body,
her pretty face with the bright cheeks, dimpled chin,
her little nose,
the brown hair dancing as she shakes her head,
her lips ready for kissing,
how he wishes he were back –

The soldier, jamming people into the car
next to his, has yelled at him.
He grabs a man who has fallen, stopping the line,
shoves him up on board,
goads the others with his gun,
an old woman, her daughter, an aged man,
not many left to load.

She's just waiting for him to finish,
to return as soon as work is done,
not even to change out of his uniform.
She says it makes him irresistible.
"You handsome man," she teases,
"Kiss me quick!"

The last man stumbles up to the cattle car.
The guard sees him, grabs him, heaves him in,
jams him into the crowd,
rams them all up tight behind the door,
pushes it shut across their flailing arms,
bangs the bar down tight with them all inside,
jumps to the ground, signals the train to move,
their screaming voices lost in the wheels' thick din.

The guard shouts, *That was the last of them.*
Hey, where are you going?
The soldier boy shouts back to the guard with a smile:
Ah, home to heaven!

A-Singing

The daily train, more or less on time,
its cattle cars rumbling up the track,
headed out over the eastern rim.
We left the camp a-singing.

Something fluttered out of a car,
floated over, then fell back
landing like a fallen star.
We left the camp a-singing.

A farmer found it on a clod
where he'd been plowing. What is this?
A postcard, with a message. Odd.
We left the camp a-singing.

Stamped, addressed, all ready to send,
he mailed the card at the postal office
intended for the sender's friend.
We left the camp a-singing.

The man who sorted the mail each day
took a look: "A ghetto address.
Those people have been taken away."
We left the camp a-singing.

The message went to the dead-letter case.
The train arrived at the getting-off place.
The smoke emerged from the furnaces.
We left the camp a-singing.

The Truth

Stuffed in a cattle car on the way
to the labor camp, I steeled myself
to remember, whatever occurred,
that I was created free, that I
would stay free in my mind, that I
would remain true to myself.

So when I saw him, a friend from school,
a year ahead, who hadn't been allowed
to graduate either, I threw my arms
around his body, then drew back —
how thin he was!

"Listen," I said, "We must not give up.
"Must keep our minds alive, stay faithful
"to the truth, our truth, real truth."

The dark hollows of his eyes seemed not
to see anything but my clothes
as if they might hide something that
could be found by his spindly hands.
Irked, I asked, "What do you want?"
The voice I heard, fervent, replied,
"Did you bring anything to eat?"

Freight Yard Telephone

I've got five box cars standing on the track.
Move them?
Who said to clear the track for the troop trains?
How long?
Because the box cars have been here two whole days!
How should I know how many are dead?
Yesterday I held them back for transport trains.
Building another camp, they said.
These cars had better have priority soon.
You won't believe the smell.
I don't have enough guards to let them out.
Or food.
Shortages? Yes, I know. Too little of everything.
Look, five cars, just let me attach them to something
coming through tomorrow.
Christ Almighty!!

Move!

They've been crushed together in their fate
as never in their lives.
A dissociated group, not knowing each other.
Strangers, forced to meet.
They now become defined by those outside:
the hated people.

Such are his thoughts, this budding theologian,
packed upright with a hundred others
in a bone-shaking box car,
the noise of its grinding wheels
beating in his ears.

Massed humanity! We must try
to care for one another.
That is what this means.
God is teaching us to love
the neighbor next to us —
I will hold you up,
keep you warm, speak comfort to you.
The ones I can reach, next to me!
You are here, God, in this car!

At last the train does stop,
The big door slowly opens,
Those who are still alive
tumble over the dead,
struggle to separate, to breathe!

The man falls to his knees, hands clasped.
A guard comes, slams his rifle butt
into the theologian's back.
Get moving!

The man struggles up.
Suddenly he sees the terrified eyes
of the others oblivious to his, to him.
He realizes,
this is not a platform for his performance.
Slowly
he reaches his feet. If God is here,
he, too, is a forced traveler.
The theologian moves on.

Flowers Await

> *In memory of Ilse Weber, a Jewish songwriter from Prague, who sang to children as she went with them into an Auschwitz gas chamber in 1944.*

Lullaby, lullaby, I am right here beside you.
Her voice melodious, gentle, and clear.
Be brave little children. Come into the room.
How could they hate these young ones so dear?
Of the flowers that bloom in the summer we'll sing.
Image them now. See the sweet joy they bring.
Come my little ones, come.

The children come to her, gathering around.
The light casts its rays on the tiniest being.
As she keeps on singing, the loveliest sound.
Let lovely sweet flowers be all you are seeing.
So soothing her voice, though her eyes fight the tears,
she lovingly holds them to quiet their fears.
Calm my little ones, calm.

Lullaby, lullaby, you will soon be asleep.
She holds them still tighter as she sees the chamber.
Don't open your eyes, O dear ones, don't peek.
The sound of the gas begins as they enter.
Now flowers await you, so tranquil, so still,
the flowers that love you, as always they will.
Sleep my little ones, sleep.
Sleep my little ones, sleep.

A Matter at the Camp

The Officer's Revolver

Where were they going?
None of them knew, trudging over the road,
which maybe led to nowhere.
Asking the soldiers only got you
a rifle butt in the back.

Even the soldiers seemed afraid,
as if they didn't know either
whether a new labor camp lay at the road's end
or a hidden ditch for killing.
They just wanted to get there.

However their officer knew.
You could tell by the way he kept his grim mouth shut,
motioning others out of the way when someone fell
so he could put a bullet in the prisoner's skull.
He never holstered his revolver.

You had to keep your mind on something pleasant
if you could think at all,
or occupy your mind with an equation,
a conundrum, a poem.
Anything as long as it didn't make you
stumble to the ground.

Love, Willie

Always signed "love, Willie,"
he wrote each week a letter home.
When the war started, he hadn't wanted to go
but so many friends had volunteered,
the Fatherland needed soldiers.
Now as he rounded up the hated ones,
he looked so handsome in his uniform.

"Don't be afraid for me, my dear," he wrote.
"I am out of the battle.
"At first I didn't care much for this job,
"but better us than them, and it gets easier.
"The first was hardest. Some of us backed out.
"But I stayed with my duty. Now the worst
"is breathing the bitter stench within the pits."

Sometimes his letters came with wonderful presents
—chocolate, jewelry, toys—
like Christmas, so it seemed to the little ones.
Always a loving father, Willie was.
His children would never suffer from these people,
whose heads exploded as he shot them down,
then tumbled them onto the others in the ditch.

Out of Order

The commandant of all the camps!
Coming here!
To see how we use our prisoners for the war!
All must be in order for his visit.
Dressed in our best uniforms,
each man stiff-standing to his task.
I welcome him myself.

Bring him to look over our books,
the daily numbers correct to the last man,
each one so many calories per day,
so many days of labor 'til they die.
Everything measured with strict accuracy.
Surely for such precision in accounts
the commandant will order promotions, even awards.

Then the commandant pukes,
pukes on the death-house floor where the used-up go.
His aides tell me I needn't be concerned:
his is a "sensitive stomach," often upset.
Relief to me! I had felt cold fear
that he had taken offense, found something wrong,
something out of order in my camp.

Peckity-Peck

He sat in his overcoat and hat
with his silk muffler round his neck,
thin lips pursed and glasses thick,
typing peckity-peckity-peck.

A thousand prisoners now a day
where there were just hundreds coming through,
to be registered, "selected" for work,
and the rest shipped where? God only knew.

They selected him because he could type,
peckity-peckity-peckity-peck.
But the hell of it was, this terrible mud
had made his exquisite shoes a wreck.

Mud from the moment he stepped outside,
mud to his barracks, muddy the floor,
mud in his bedding, even the shack
was tracked where he sat with mud some more.

And the broken-down stove in the squalid room
worked on and off, more often off.
His fingers flew on the freezing keys.
Peckity-peckity-peckity-*cough*.

Finally the coughs outnumbered the pecks.
They hauled him down to a waiting throng
for the gas, the ovens. *Will someone clean
my beautiful shoes?* Then he was gone.

Moment of Glory

The rain lets up. Not even the heavy smoke
obscures the sudden brightness of the sun,
which strikes the solitary tree so that it shines
in the late afternoon's ethereal light.
Strange picture: the emaciated man
in his striped gown, just gazing at the tree,
looking out beyond the thick barbed wire
where they have cleared the ground around the camp.

*The light, the light – I have never seen the light
so golden . . . .*

Leaves turn glittery, dancing on the branches,
gilded as if the tree had been made over
for the pleasure of the gods
just at twilight, as the dark clouds part,
as the sun pours out over the hills
where in a moment of glory before it's gone,
the entire landscape gleams, shines in the light.

So golden . . . .

The shout comes over his shoulder: *Hey, get moving!
There's more waiting for you to load back there.
Lazy oaf!*

The man's own bones ache in the growing dark,
but he resumes unloading his corpse-filled cart,
dumping the bodies down in the burial ditch.
Then, like the others, he goes for another load.
The bodies never run out, or so it seems.
Yet he knows the end of the day will finally come.
Then sleep — that's what he's counting on —
dreaming of golden light.

Camp Cant

Why in a world of irritations
—the pain of standing at the workbenches all day,
wretched dirty-looking soup to eat,
cuffs from the guards at the barracks,
slats to sleep on without blankets in the cold night—
why should she annoy me, this little girl,
in her twenties maybe, always going on to us
about God's plan for us, God's holy goodness.

"Does God wear jackboots?" I asked her once.
But I'm too tired for any argument.
Anyway, who cares? She does no harm.
Let her believe whatever makes her happy.
Happiness for me is ten minutes with the moon
on the way back after the long workday.

The moon that has shone for millions of years,
changes shapes, plays skip-to-my-Lou among the clouds.
I love the moon.
It does not see me out of its shadowy face,
nor does it hear from me when I want hope.
It just is, and shines when I get to see it,
a great indifference in the sky.
I wish to live because life's what I am,
but all I really want is a warm, comfortable bed,
a bowl of good hot nourishing soup,
maybe a nip of something with alcohol in it,
and a view of the gentle moon.

Shining Eyes

He likes to see the young boys laugh and shout
out on the playing fields. He remembers now
how good they looked, chasing the soccer ball.
A kick, a goal! Then all embraced in glee.
He can barely see the far-off field
beyond the heavy fence but he remembers
the brightness in their eyes.

Strange he should remember them so well.
Not the dull-eyed others in the camp.
Not the hard-eyed guards. Nor the angry eyes
of those who might have caught him watching.
Nor the impassive eyes of the already dead.
He survived that life, saved when the alien
foreign soldiers came, their eyes amazed.

Such a long time ago, those soccer players
—"Vigorous Youth"—being prepared for war.
But how does he remember?
How could he even have seen a soccer field?
Can he have imagined it happening?
Something wonderful to keep him living?
Something to keep the brightness in his eyes?

Purple and Gold

Past the guard-tower, out where the barbed-wire ends,
a field of lupine, flowers in purple and gold.
She gazes at them longingly, every morning at dawn,
as she walks with the others to work,
to work,
and she dreams, as she walks, of the many people she knew
to whom she would hand a bright bouquet of flowers,
people who worked at the forced-labor camp with her,
who then would smile at her,
at work,
making munitions to wage the horror of war.

Then one day as she makes her way with the others
to work, she sees him, the guard come down from the tower,
makes his way past the sharpened rolls of barbed wire
to the beautiful lupine field,
the field,
and taking his bayonet, cuts loose a few,
for whom, she does not know, perhaps a lover,
perhaps a little child, perhaps his own,
or perhaps a grave in a field,
a field,
where the dead do not have to get up, go make war.

Christmas!

Red wrappings, bright greenery, everywhere.
Logs flaming in the fireplace.
Now the family gathers around the table,
the gleaming goose,
mounds of white mashed potatoes
steaming under lakes of gravy,
cranberries, celery, olives, squash
waiting on the plates.

Thank you O Father
for thy many blessings,
for our family all together,
for the warmth and comfort
of our home,
for the —
Telephone!

Father rises, strides through the double doors
of the dining room into the hall.

Hello. Yes . . .
Three of them . . . ?
Yes . . . yes . . .
When you find them? Hold them . . . .
We must find out how they got out.
Yes . . . no, I'm not coming in.

He returns, announces:
A matter at the camp.
I'll take care of it tomorrow.
Come, let us rejoice!
Then their feast begins.

Outside,
over the snowy road at the camp's rear
uniformed men track down the missing prisoners,
who beg to be shot rather than taken back.

What's Left?

"I Join the Gulls"
A pastiche of lines from diaries and letters that Etty Hillesum of Amsterdam wrote in Nazi camps until her death at age 29 in Auschwitz in 1943.

"The heath outside
 is vast and rolling as the sea."
"A rainbow over the camp, the sun
shines in the mud puddles."

"I join the gulls in their movement through the skies,"
"black and silver birds,
among the massive deep-blue clouds."
"Ah, children, we live in a strange world . . . ."

"If only we could keep a feeling
for their rhythm, rising so high above."
We'd be "lighter and more liberated
than ever before . . . ."

"One would have to be a very great poet
to describe them."
"Ah, my dearest friend,"
"it's a complete madhouse here . . . ."

Maximum Capacity

Basically the vans are a technical matter.
    You
         have to keep things moving
at high speed.
        No hitches.
             And orderly,
each phase leading seamlessly
        to the next.
    For example
        loading the vans
to the max reduces the vehicle's stability.
    Normal load
        is nine to the square yard.
            However,
during the operation
        they tend to rush
    toward the rear door.
            Therefore
the back axle may become overloaded.

One should not eliminate lights inside
    though seldom used
           because
in the darkness
    when the door closes
        screaming occurs.
Also
    fit the draining hole
        with a slanting trap
for easy cleaning afterwards.

                                          (continued)

On the way in,
    take away and quickly shoot
        those who catch on
lest they start panic.

When you arrive,
    make the undressing room
look like
        an "information station"
with signs saying,
        "Clean is Good!"
Let the gas,
    be poured in
        by a
"disinfection squad."
That way they won't know
    until
        it's way too late.
That way
    You won't lose time.
        That way,
there need be no down time
        at the ovens.
That way, you can handle
    1,800 people per day.
        Dead is good!

Dreams

Some dream of pleasant things:
their wives, their kids,
images flitting through escaping brains.

Others dream the dreadful:
what happened to their wives, their kids,
after they were taken away.

Still others dream of ordinary things:
their work, the other prisoners,
the prisoner on the bunk slats next to theirs

whose face suddenly becomes a dog's,
snarling, vicious — he tries to scream
but makes no sound, the way it is in dreams,

cannot get it out of his open throat,
flails about to wake the other prisoners
only to find a dog's face, every one.

A fellow prisoner wakes him up:
Shut up. I want to sleep.
You're having a nightmare.

He sits up, looks at him, looks at the others
whom the noise had awakened,
every one, snarling — a dog's head.

His body convulses, he screeches — wham!
He does not know what hit him
or who,

or who gets him up in the morning,
or how he gets to work,
or why the guards laugh at the sight of him.

He dares not look at their faces
for fear that every one might bear
that same snarling head.

"O'er the Green Valley"

They found out he could sing
so they pulled him out from the working prisoners
that they were guarding, told him,
"Sing a song, little rat."
It would pass the afternoon.

Full of fear, he felt he couldn't sing,
tears in his eyes, a choking in his throat,
but they were tenacious: "You *will* sing."
And so he sang, a cheery little tune,
despite the crying in his heart.

> "O'er the green valley I rove, I rove,
> Until I shall find you my love,
> Waiting for me in the golden grove,
> Under the heavens above."

"More, more!" they insisted, cheering,
so he sang another verse, then another,
all through the beautiful afternoon,
while the other prisoners moved another two thousand
bodies to the ovens for burning.

Blood, Worms, Piss, Shit, Vomit

The corpses just piled up.
Yet the trains kept coming.
They were cleaning out the ghetto.
The head men ordered it.
"You have to take on more!"

We prisoners, forced to pull the bodies
out of the gas rooms after death,
broke down as the stench grew greater.
The ovens could not take them fast enough.
The corpses just piled up.

Those condemned to die just stood around,
guarded, waiting for space in the gas chambers.
Some of them slit their wrists, their throats.
We knew, we wept, we worked on,
but the trains kept coming.

We kept throwing the bodies onto piles
waiting for the smoking ovens.
Underneath the stacks, a cesspool formed,
filled with blood, worms, piss, shit, vomit.
Still the corpses just piled up.

We couldn't keep on. Some of us stopped,
preferring to be shot,
which only added to the waiting bodies.
Yet no relief,
the trains just kept on coming.

We yearned for the end of the day,
for a few hours of sweet sleep.
But even in our dreams, especially in our dreams,
the trains — *the trains* — just kept on coming,
and the corpses — *the corpses* — just piled up.

Revolt

He tossed around on the hard slats in the dark room,
trying to figure it out. Why should they wait?

Hundred of prisoners stuffed in narrow barracks.
The guards? — just two, one at each end's door.

Half asleep, but machine guns in their hands.
Yes, some of the prisoners would be shot.

But hundreds rushing two in the quiet night?
Revolt spreading in barracks throughout the camp?

Thousands then rushing the towers, the gates, the guards.
They could not kill so many. Numbers are strength!

Spread the word. All prisoners. Three nights hence.
Next day the message began from man to man.

Back from their forced labor outside the camp
they lined up near their barracks for the count.

Then an officer in his handsome coat
walked to the prisoner who'd planned it out —

Numbers are strength! —
and shot him dead.

The prisoner who had reported this revolt
did not return to the dead man's barracks room.

He'd traded his information for a spot
on an upper tier of the racks in another place,

out from under the dysentery, vomit,
that dripped down from the prisoners up above.

They talked of revolt no more.

Three Minutes

Too young for slave labor,
cuffed aside to go find derelicts,
smelly stiffs who'd died in the night
in the stockade's barracks.
He sucked in wind against the stench,
entered, probed for corpses
on rows of slats where prisoners flopped to sleep.

Hated the faces
until one stopped him cold.
Emaciated, no light in the eyes,
but chin, nose, eyebrows—no doubt
his father. Did not cry, just slouched,
brushed off grime, untangled hair,
then drug him out to the guard at the donkey cart.

"Stack him on, you little shit!"
Placed face upright, folded arms, then said.
"I want to go where you bury them."
Guard's thin lips quivered
but he saw, he knew.
"Climb up, damn you.
"Three minutes—all you'll get for funeral time."

You Get Used to Anything

The field bordered the camp.
There the prisoners worked
right next to the barbed wire.

It seemed as if the barbed wire could speak,
could make the sounds of screaming,
so loud as he worked, they filled his head.

Kept screaming, no matter how hard he chopped,
biting the earth with his hoe,
obliterating weeds.

To glance, to steal a look at the screaming
coming from beyond the barbed wire barrier,
could get you killed.

Once, twice, when the guards weren't watching,
He sneaked a look,
saw people screaming, shot.

So loud, so heart-rending,
as if the air around him, full of screams.
He chopped frantically, crying.

He chopped wildly, holding onto his hoe
while swinging it in the air
to stop the screaming.

He couldn't stand it,
the screaming, the awful sound.
But after a while, he began to get used to it.

"You get used to anything,
even screaming," they told him
back in the barracks at night.

Back in the field, hoeing,
he almost did get used to the screaming,
almost could totally shut it out.

After the war when the camp was captured
he did not believe the screaming had ever happened.
No, it was simply impossible.

He had simply imagined it.
Something inside him had died, the screaming,
something that thought of it.

He didn't think of it
except when he woke in the middle of the night
chopping, killing, screaming.

Black Smoke

Didn't he understand the need?
The longer they breathed, the more the problem.
The Army had to live off the land.
Why feed all these hated people?

In desperation, he looked out
of his office window. Heaving black smoke
from the ovens spoke of devouring speed.
How could they take them faster yet?

Ingeniousness of the master race!
He tried to keep up his confidence.
At first they'd assembled captives in batches.
Firing squads shot them into ditches.

Still too slow! Too inefficient!
Make them kneel on the brim of the pits.
Fire a shell at the base of each skull.
Topple them over into the ditch.

He'd tried it all: Made them dig the ditch.
Some died just from the work itself.
Made them lie down before being shot
on the bodies of the already dead.

The numbers of daily deaths increased,
rose again when the guns arrived,
machine guns downing hundreds at once.
Still the captives kept coming in.

At last, the gas and the cremation ovens!
No bullets, no more ditches to dig.
Corpses reduced to smoke and ash.
Now they could execute so many more!

He could see it coming—medals, applause,
triumphant speeches, his picture among
the heroes of history—the master of death!
They found him next to his discharged gun.

In the Barracks

blood
on my thighs

soldiers
pull up their pants

they leave
not looking back

I don't feel
my body

I just want
to be alone

I just want
the dark to return

I just want
the dark

A Penitential Prayer

Shivering in the Ditch

Ferocious explosions, evergreens uprooted,
clumps of churned up, turned-over, broken limbs,
air still thick with pieces of branches, dirt.
The boy, head down, lies shivering in the ditch
at the crater's edge. "Stay put" they shouted.
"Bombs do not hit the same place twice."
Many of them subsequently died.

At night, the great bombs stop.
Everything settles.
His quivering body pushes against debris.
He wants to go home but he has seen the tanks
blast houses down, heard his parents scream.
Silence now. Not even cricket voices.
A burning smell in the thick, still-filthy air.

He will survive with the rifle found among
the dead. A shaking boy who joins the troops
when they come counter-attacking back, the one
who hangs around the field canteen in hope
of a hunk of bread, the one who doesn't seem
quite right, the one who cries when the enemy comes,
the one who only when shooting seems at peace.

Then We'd Hear a Shot

No one said anything, but after a time,
a few made their way one by one to the back garden.
Then we'd hear a shot, then another.
I didn't know what to do.
Father was among the first to go out.
He looked so grand in his uniform, a general,
the medal at his throat.

So I rose, too, just eleven years old,
walked to the door that led to the back garden,
stepped outside into the bright sunshine.
The sun shone on the flowers that had come up early,
shone on the greening grass, the budding bushes,
shone on the bodies lying here and there
of those who had gone out.

I realized that father was among them.
I didn't know what to say.
Then an older boy, sitting on a garden bench,
called to me. "Come sit here."
The air smelled warm, like a bakery, and a bird sang.
We talked about whether there would still be
school to go to anymore.

Free?

One day they gathered all who could walk, started marching them
 to the west.
Only those too sick to walk stayed in the bunks, some already
 dead.
Living skeletons, aching bones, slack muscles, bodies a wreck.
Durchfall, they call this dysentery, took it in bedpans, threw it out.
Then some of us noticed—the guards, the dogs, all gone.

At first, we just stayed in our bunks, waiting, watching.
Then we began to look out—no guards, no dogs, could we go?
It's a trick, you go out, dogs bark, then starts the shooting.
Suddenly soldiers in different uniforms appeared, we hid.
"Come out, you are free, we've come to liberate you!"

The door burst open, young men, soldiers, entered, looking
 aghast.
The dead, the sick on the bunks, excrement everywhere, the
 stench.
They stare at us, tears appear on their faces. We show only fear.
More soldiers come, some give us water, bread, carry us out.
We gulp the bread, then vomit outside as they take us to big
 trucks.

Red crosses, not swastikas, some of us stumble toward the camp
 gate.
"Hey, come back, we want to help!" The soldiers catch the run-
 aways.
Most of us are too sick to run, don't know anyway where to go.
In the moving truck, I close my eyes, try to feel free but cannot.
They take us to a place where there's soup and doctors to look us
 over.

Several die on the way. I wonder, what am I doing here?
Why haven't I died? I could not grasp what they were trying to
 tell me.
Hundreds of camps like mine. Thousands were worked to death,
left to starve, or gassed, then fed to the ovens, black smoke.
My family, my home, all gone. Why am I still alive?

Free?
When I close my eyes, the terrible camp comes back.
Will I ever be free of that? Of the people who died?
I was almost dead when the soldiers rescued me.
I suppose I should be glad.

Great Parade

To her, how clear the images stand out,
thousands of girls, yet each seems still alive.
Her photo shows them in school uniforms,
whose buttons glint so brightly in the light,
awaiting a parade. Glee fills their faces—
such excitement!—each wags a tiny flag.
The picture: A mass of swastikas.

Could she imagine how this scene would end?
Little time remained for gaiety.
Work for the State's outpouring war must come:
assembling shells, making tanks and planes,
knitting socks at home, and growing food.
No, she would want to forget all that
in later days.

In time they were getting messages of the dead:
fathers, husbands, brothers. Then bombs dropped,
blowing up homes, hers among them, leaving
dead in the rubble. But she survived,
and so did these small things—the photograph, the flags.
What innocence! What joy! A great parade!
A truly shining time!

Dung Buckets

In the drab camp she thought a lot about
her chosen vocation before they had come to get her,
the still-lives she had painted, bowls of flowers,
pretty, almost saintly, shy and chaste.
Never, however, would she paint again
as before this misery. Could she paint at all?

Women, thin, in worn-out prison shifts,
bearing buckets of dung from the base latrine
to spread outside to fertilize fields of wheat
for feeding the army. In the labor camp
they ate gray scraps of slop in watery soup.
Would there be for them an "again"?

But "again" came; the camp—liberated!
She resumed painting, not little pots of flowers
but gorgeous landscapes of ebullient blooms,
hundreds of bursting buds in brilliant hues:
reds, yellows, oranges, the height of brightness,
as though she must try to find the sun again.

Sewers

Fourteen months in the sewers of the city,
terrorized by the troops, hidden,
underground, no sun,
stench penetrating, dark, damp,
clogged nostrils, shit in one's throat,
watery overflow daily flooded.
You can't imagine.

Dirt, rats, disease, fights,
if the troops despised the hiding hated people,
why was it not enough
simply to drive them underground?
Were they so eager to shoot,
to leave no one alive?
To live meant to defy?

He walked on, thinking of the sewer.
How time had snatched so many friends,
even those not murdered.
How to find the way out
of the shit-sewer in his mind?
One can never forget
the way back in.

Why Ask Me?

At the beginning we didn't even know about the end.
So why ask me about it?

Yes, I was second in command of the district in Warsaw.
My degree was new, I needed a job, it was a job.

Why don't you ask me about the job I have now,
the job I have held for some twenty years?

I'm with a mountaineering publishing house.
I write mountain guide books, publish a climber's magazine.

I have a significant job, I'm expert in the field.
That job with the district, just two or so years, end of the war.

What do I even remember? Nothing.
I had no power anyway. Just a bureaucrat.

I encourage people now to take joy in the mountains,
the pure air, the bright sun, the scenery's beauty.

As we say now, "Joy through Beauty!
What did we say before? How should I know?

Joy, beauty, that's what I think about now.
The ghetto is just dust gone, long long ago.

Great Goethe

Preserve? Memorial? This despicable camp?
Bulldoze over it, is what I say.
I've lived here all my life, it's a nice town.
I don't want it scarred by obscenity.
We're better off not even to remember.

Don't you know that this is where Goethe came?
Stayed one summer, wrote a poem here.
If you would do anything with that patch of ground,
put a statue of him in the middle of it,
there where you say the ovens used to be.

Let flowers cover it up, plant colorful shrubs,
with a sign that says, "Great Goethe lingered here,
wrote poems, bringing to all the whirling world
the joy that he perceived upon this spot."
That's what we really need to cheer us up.

But no, here where the great man probably walked
you want to contaminate his memory
by mixing it with all the scruffy rabble
who came from someplace else to die in piles.
Pray God to save their souls—then get on out!

In Place of Explanation

"There, far off to the right, where the trains came in.
There, the platform where the slats came off the doors
of the cattle cars, stampedes began.
People stumbled out through a jumble of dead.
Uniformed guards whipped out the living,
assembled them over the way at the sorting place,
chose those who could work, then pushed the rest like beasts,
shot the stragglers. There where the trees are now
—you can scarcely see—down into a kind of funnel,
leading through two doors to the gas chambers.
Farther along that way gaped the waiting ovens.
After an interval of time, slave laborers
threw in the bodies that had just been gassed
until black smoke terrified the sky.
Well, you get the idea, that's the gist."

Every place he pointed, there now appeared
nothing but green peace, gentle vegetation,
swaying in the straying winds of the amiable afternoon.
Leafy trees, bright bushes, lush grass, soft ground,
bereft of buildings, ovens, gas traps, stations, trains,
guns, clubs, and so many screaming people.
Why try to bring it up again?

Because it was.

Otherwise, we might give in
to the power to paint bright pigments over horror
or look away as nature conspires to hide.
Even the reach for reasons leads
into the pit of unreason in which
millions of voices beg for a way to explain
their deaths.
In place of explanation I offer
this penitential prayer for the living,
these lamentations for the dead.

Photo by Rebecca Curtis Photography.

Gerald George felt his interest in the Holocaust become an obsession as he tried to make sense of a disaster in which six million people perished. He began writing poems about it, not to explain it but to keep it from becoming a statistic, to imagine individuals who endured it, including those who let it happen. He sees his book as penitential, in effect a prayer.

He has previously published two books of poetry: *Figments* and *Imitations of Indonesia and Other Poems*. He has also published poetry in numerous periodicals and anthologies, and his verse play Bailey's Mistake was performed in Maine's 2008 One-Act Play Festival. He served on the editorial board of the literary journal *Off the Coast*, and for several years he coordinated the annual Roque Bluffs Poetry Festival. He and his wife Carol live in Belfast, Maine, USA.

www.ingramcontent.com/pod-product-compliance
Lightning Source LLC
Chambersburg PA
CBHW030532080526
44586CB00011B/406